First World War
and Army of Occupation
War Diary
France, Belgium and Germany

21 DIVISION
Divisional Troops
'A' Squadron South Irish Horse
11 September 1915 - 31 May 1916

WO95/2141/1

The Naval & Military Press Ltd
www.nmarchive.com
Published in association with The National Archives

Published by

The Naval & Military Press Ltd

Unit 10 Ridgewood Industrial Park,

Uckfield, East Sussex,

TN22 5QE England

Tel: +44 (0) 1825 749494

www.naval-military-press.com

www.nmarchive.com

This diary has been reprinted in facsimile from the original. Any imperfections are inevitably reproduced and the quality may fall short of modern type and cartographic standards.

© Crown Copyright
Images reproduced by permission of The National Archives, London, England, 2015.

Contents

Document type	Place/Title	Date From	Date To
Heading	WO95/2141/1 "A" Squadron South Irish No.		
Heading	21 Div Troops "A" Sqn Sth Irish Horse Sept 1915-May 1916 (To 15 Corps) 1880		
Heading	21st Division "A" Squadron S. Irish Horse Vol I Sept 15		
Heading	War Diary Of "A" Sq South Irish Horse From Sept 11 1915 Sept 30 1915 Volume I		
War Diary	Southampton	11/09/1915	11/09/1915
War Diary	Havre	12/09/1915	12/09/1915
War Diary	St. Omer	13/09/1915	13/09/1915
War Diary	Watten	14/09/1915	20/09/1915
War Diary	Blaringhem	21/09/1915	21/09/1915
War Diary	Lespresses	22/09/1915	22/09/1915
War Diary	Ferfay	23/09/1915	24/09/1915
War Diary	Labuissiere	25/09/1915	25/09/1915
War Diary	Philosophe	26/09/1915	26/09/1915
War Diary	42 Miles S.E. Sailly L A Bourse	27/09/1915	28/09/1915
War Diary	Bethune	29/09/1915	30/09/1915
Heading	21st Division "A" Squadron S. Irish Horse Vol II Oct 15		
Heading	War Diary of "A" Sqd South Irish Horse from October 1st to October 31st 1915		
War Diary	Aire	01/10/1915	01/10/1915
War Diary	Morbeque	02/10/1915	02/10/1915
War Diary	Strazeele	03/10/1915	31/10/1915
Heading	21st Division "A" Sq. S. Irish Horse Vol 3 Nov 15		
Heading	War Diary of "A" Sqd South Irish Horse From Nov 1st 1915 to Nov 30 1915 Vol I		
War Diary	Strazeele	01/11/1915	30/11/1915
Heading	21st Div "A" Squadron S. Irish Horse Vol 4		
Heading	War Diary of "A" Sqd South Irish Horse From Dec 1st 1915 to Dec 31st 1915 Vol I		
War Diary	Strazeele	01/12/1915	31/12/1915
Heading	21st Divisional Cavalry "A" Squadron South Irish Horse January 1916		
Heading	A Sq. S. Irish Horse Vol 5		
Heading	War Diary of "A" Sqd. South Irish Horse From Jan 1st 1916 to Jan 31st 1916 Vol I		
War Diary	Strazeele	01/01/1916	31/01/1916
Heading	21st Divisional Cavalry "A" Squadron South Irish Horse February 1916		
Heading	A. Squad S.I. Horse 21st Div Vol 6		
Heading	War Diary "A" Sqd South Irish Horse From Feb 1st 1916 to Feb 29th 1916		
War Diary	Strazeele	01/02/1916	29/02/1916
Heading	21st Divisional Cavalry "A" Squadron South Irish Horse March 1916		
Heading	A S.I. Horse Vol 7		
Heading	War Diary "A" Sqd South Irish Horse From March 1st 1916 to March 31st 1916		

War Diary	Strazeele	01/03/1916	31/03/1916
Heading	21st Divisional Cavalry Became Part Of XV Corps Cavalry In May 1916 "A" Squadron South Irish Horse April 1916		
War Diary	Strazeele	01/04/1916	02/04/1916
War Diary	Ribemont	02/04/1916	30/04/1916
Heading	21st Divisional Cavalry XV Corps Cavalry Left 21st Division & Joined XV Corps 14.5.16 "A" Squadron South Irish Horse May 1916		
Heading	War Diary of "A" Sqd South Irish Horse May 1st 1916 To May 31st 1916		
War Diary	Ribemont	01/05/1916	11/05/1916
War Diary	In Lines Holy Way Between Ribemont & Heilly	12/05/1916	31/05/1916

WO 95/2141/1

'A' Squadron South Irish Horse

~~21ST DIVISION~~

21 DIV TROOPS ~~+ CORPS TRPS~~

'A' SQN STH IRISH HORSE

SEP 1915 – MAY 1916

(TO 15 CORPS)

1880

121/
7517

21st Burnin

"A" Squadron 21st Horse
Vol I.
Sept 15

Army Form C. 2118.

WAR DIARY
or
INTELLIGENCE SUMMARY.
(Erase heading not required.)

Confidential

WAR Diary
of
"A" Sq. SOUTH. IRISH. HORSE

from Sept 11" 1915   Sept 30" 1915

Volume I

Army Form C. 2118.

WAR DIARY
or
INTELLIGENCE SUMMARY.

(Erase heading not required.)

Instructions regarding War Diaries and Intelligence Summaries are contained in F. S. Regs., Part II. and the Staff Manual respectively. Title pages will be prepared in manuscript.

Place	Date	Hour	Summary of Events and Information	Remarks and references to Appendices
SOUTHAMPTON	11/9/15	7.30 P.M	Sailed with 135 men 6 officers 145 horses per S/S ANGLO CANADIAN.	
HAVRE	12/9/15	10 A.M.	Arrived HAVRE 10. A.M. disembarked. Remained on quay until 6. P.M. Train entrained for St OMER.	
St OMER	13/9/15	4. P.M	Arrived St OMER. Marched to WATTEN arriving there about 9. P.M. Billeted men & horses	
WATTEN	14/9/15		Billeted at WATTEN resting.	
do	15/9/15		do Training. Grenades.	
do	16/9/15		do	
do	17/9/15		do	
do	18/9/15		do	
do	19/9/15		do	
do	20/9/15		Left WATTEN. 6. P.M. marched to BLARINGHEM. arrived 2.30 A.M. Bivouaced in a field.	N.C.F.
BLARINGHEM	21/9/15		Left BLARINGHEM. 6.30. P.M. marched to FERFAY LES PRESSES. arrived 9. P.M. Bivouaced.	
LES PRESSES	22/9/15		Left LES PRESSES. 6.30. P.M. marched to FERFAY at FERFAY.	
FERFAY	23/9/15		At FERFAY. 6.M.	
do	24/9/15		Left FERFAY. 6. P.M. marched to LABUISSIERE arr 10 P.M.	
LABUISSIERE	25/9/15		Left LABUISSIERE. 3. P.M. marched via NOEUX-LES-MINES & MAZINGARBE to PHILOSOPHE, arr 9. P.M. very wet-dark	N.C.F.

WAR DIARY

INTELLIGENCE SUMMARY.

Army Form C. 2118.

Instructions regarding War Diaries and Intelligence Summaries are contained in F. S. Regs., Part II. and the Staff Manual respectively. Title pages will be prepared in manuscript.

(Erase heading not required.)

Place	Date	Hour	Map ref FRANCE SHEET 36.C. 1:8,000 Summary of Events and Information	Remarks and references to Appendices
PHILOSOPHE	26/9/15		Moved to "L" at 3. A.M. Officers were put on traffic control at PHILOSOPHE during morning. About noon two officers Lieut. C.S. KIRK & 2nd Lieut N. ANDERSON were sent for by 21st D.H. Q to accompany Gen up to the trenches at G.22.B. Met FRANCE sheet 36.C. 1:40,000 about 11.30 A.M. Two shrapnel burst one on each side of Bgd about 50 yds away. At 5.P.M. I moved Bgd about half a mile N.W. in direction of SAILLY LA BOURSE. as being close to guns is not the best place for cavalry to have their lines. At 2.30 A.M. I got orders to move again to a plot hay a mile nearer SAILLY LA BOURSE. At about 8.P.M. I got orders to send three officers to make a reconnaissance of roads running from G.15.C.8.4. to G.28.10.5 and back by G.22 to G.16.C.03 & back to G.15.C.8.4. Very wet day. Officers doing police duty till 30 men.	
½ miles S.E. SAILLY LA BOURSE	27/9/15			N.C.7
do	28/9/15		awaiting orders to move. received orders 6 P.M. to move at 9 P.M. Very heavy rain all night. Marched to BETHUNE & arr. here 12.30 A.M. bivouced in Meadow horses in Bynack in lines. Very wet.	

Army Form C. 2118.

WAR DIARY
or
INTELLIGENCE SUMMARY.
(Erase heading not required.)

Place	Date	Hour	Summary of Events and Information	Remarks and references to Appendices
BETHUNE	29/9/15		Orders to march at 2.30 P.M. to AIRE. 7.30 P.M. Horses in lines in field & men billeted.	
do	30/9/15		At AIRE, Camp routine.	
do	"		Signed Noel Furlong Capt. R.H.A. O.C. "A" Sqdn 1st K Horse	

21st Division

121/7517

"A" Squadron L. Strike Horse
Vol II
Oct. 15

Army Form C. 2118.

WAR DIARY
or
INTELLIGENCE SUMMARY.

(Erase heading not required.)

Confidential
War Diary
of
"A" Sqd South Irish Horse
from October 1st to October 31st 1915

WAR DIARY
or
INTELLIGENCE SUMMARY.
(Erase heading not required.)

Army Form C. 2118.

Place	Date	Hour	Summary of Events and Information	Remarks and references to Appendices
AIRE	1/10/15		Orders to march at 7.30 A.M, marched to MORBECQUE billeted horses in field	
MORBECQUE	2/10/15		Orders to march at 8. AM, marched via HAZEBROUCK to STRAZEELE. Billeted in large farm. Horses in field.	
STRAZEELE	3/10/15		Camp Routine, arranging billets etc.	
do	4/10/15		General Clean up after week continued marching	
	5/10/15		Squadron Parade	
	6/10/15		Exercise. Rifle & Saddle inspection by O/C	
	7/10/15		Small instructional scheme. outposts & Montup etc	
	8/10/15		Squadron Parade	
	9/10/15		Exercise, Stables etc. Football for men in afternoon	
	10/10/15		Church Parade	
	11/10/15		Squadron Parade	
	12/10/15		Exercise. Camp Routine. Pay for Squadron	
	13/10/15		Took Sqd into BAILLEUL to Corps Baths	
	14/10/15		Rifle, Saddle, &c inspection by O/C	
	15/10/15		Four Officers made report on billeting available in area	N.C.P.

WAR DIARY
or
INTELLIGENCE SUMMARY.
(Erase heading not required.)

Army Form C. 2118.

Place	Date	Hour	Summary of Events and Information	Remarks and references to Appendices
STRAZEELE	14/10/15		Our Interpreter M. Paul Ninguss was taken from us to 28th Div. M. Bousquier came in his place. Preceded to Camp routine, Squadron Parade.	
	17/10/15		Lieut Fitzherbert went to Ennequin Wood TERDENGHEM for a weeks course of instruction. Said Squadron	
	18/10/15			
	19/10/15		Changed two officers horses for better ones. Rifle & saddle inspection by OC. Mounted Sports	
	20/10/15			
	21/10/15		Sqd went to 2nd Corps baths at BAILLEUL Squadron Parade.	
	22/10/15			
	23/10/15		Went to La Motte au Bois to get timber. Lieut Fitzherbert returned. Farrier & Rifle & saddle inspection, by OC. Church parade	
	24/10/15			
	25/10/15		Squadron Parade. Bomb instruction	
	26/10/15		Exercise. Camp routine.	
	27/10/15		H.M. The King inspects the 2 Corps: Sqd represents by 1 officer & 30 men. Also 1 off & 25 men on police duty at CAESTRE. & 1 off & 23 men on police duty at BAILLEUL	H.E.F.

1577 Wt.W10791/1773 500,000 1/15 D.D.&L. A.D.S.S./Forms/C. 2118.

Place	Date	Hour	Summary of Events and Information	Remarks and references to Appendices
STEENBECQUE	29/10/15		Exercise & Camp routine. Div. Consider changing our wheels. Go & inspect seven farms. Find none as suitable as our present one.	
	30/10/15		Capt Wardell, Lieut Kent, 2ndLieut Anderson Go for a one day Course of bombing at 2ndCorps School of Grenades at TERDINGHEM.	
	31/10/15		Camp routine. Church Parade.	

Noel Sutton.
Capt. A / Adj?
O/C 6thInst Horse

A.Sq. S. Ind. Horse
rd: 3

8044/121

21st Kurram

Nov 15

Army Form C. 2118.

WAR DIARY
or
INTELLIGENCE SUMMARY.
(*Erase heading not required.*)

Confidential

War Diary

of

"A" Sqⁿ South Irish Horse

From Nov 1ˢᵗ 1915   To Nov 30ᵗʰ 1915

Vol. I

Army Form C. 2118.

WAR DIARY
or
INTELLIGENCE SUMMARY.

(Erase heading not required.)

"A" Sqd. South Irish Horse
21st Div.

Instructions regarding War Diaries and Intelligence Summaries are contained in F. S. Regs. Part II. and the Staff Manual respectively. Title pages will be prepared in manuscript.

Place	Date	Hour	Summary of Events and Information	Remarks and references to Appendices
STRAZEELE	1/11/15		Very wet. Exercise. Bomb instruction in afternoon. Capt. WARDELL. Corpl. RODMAN to KINARMOUNT. Go to II Corps Grenade School for a week's course of instruction.	
	2/11/15		Very wet. Sqd. Parade. Instruction in Catapult bombing.	N.C.P.
	3/11/15		Exercise. Sword drill in afternoon.	
	4/11/15		Fine day. Sqd. Parade. Bomb instruction. Reported to me that Capt. WARDELL has been evacuated to 1 Amb. to II Corps Grenade School with jaundice.	
	5/11/15		Exercise. Accident at II Corps Grenade School. Capt. RODMAN wounded in foot. Div. decides Sqd. to remain in present billets for week.	
	6/11/15		Snowstorm. Camp routine. Capt. WARDELL evacuated to BASE. Capt. C. R. KIRK and 30 men. Horses to to ARMENTIERES for police duty.	
	7/11/15		Church Parade. Camp routine.	
	8/11/15		Exercise. Instruction of N.C.O.'s in compass bearings etc. Sqd. Parade. Physical drill.	
	9/11/15		Fine day. Sqd. Parade. Trot over. 2 7/am. Moved 32 men & horses into it.	N.C.P.
	10/11/15		Exercise. Begin building shelters for horses	

Army Form C. 2118.

WAR DIARY
INTELLIGENCE SUMMARY.
(Erase heading not required.) A Sqd 100TH. IRISH. Horse. 7¹ Div.

Instructions regarding War Diaries and Intelligence Summaries are contained in F.S. Regs., Part II. and the Staff Manual respectively. Title pages will be prepared in manuscript.

Place	Date	Hour	Summary of Events and Information	Remarks and references to Appendices
STRAZEELE	12/1/15		Exercise. building sheltes. very wet & stormy	
	13		do and Court House	
	14		Church parade. Camp routine.	
	15		Sqd Parade. building shelters. Cook house. Latrines &c	
	16		Watering rats do do	
	17		Exercise do do	
	18		Capt FURLONG & Lieut FITZHERBERT visited ARMENTIERES to inspect Capt KIRK. This troop, who are doing police duty there. Capt FURLONG & Lieut FITZHERBERT. return from ARMENTIERES having arranged that Lieut ANDERSON is to proceed to ARMENTIERES on following monday to commence a course of instruction to Grenade & Catapult bombing	
	19		Sqd Exercise. Continue building. Found case of Scarlet Fever in Capt FURLONGS & Lieut VERNONS billet. a child was informed. Feed and 50-Div. took necessary precautions. Exercise continues. Moved to fresh billet (Capt FURLONG & Lieut VERNON)	
	20		Sqd Exercise. Continue building. very cold wind	

Army Form C. 2118.

WAR DIARY
or
INTELLIGENCE SUMMARY. "A" Sqd. SOUTH IRISH HORSE
(Erase heading not required.)

Place	Date	Hour	Summary of Events and Information	Remarks and references to Appendices
STRAZEELE	21/1/15		Church Parade. Camp scouting	
	22		Sqd. Parade. Continue building leaves great	
	23		Sqd. Parade. Physical Drill. S/S Willaby goes on leave	
	24		a little rain. Exercise. Sword Drill.	
	25		Fine day. Sqd. Parade. Football match in afternoon	
	26		Exercise. Very cold. a little snow. Bomb instruction	
	27		Heavy frost. Very cold. Exercise. Physical drill	
	28		Heavy frost. Church Parade. Camp scouting	
	29		Very cold. Training. Sqd Parade. Lieut Anderson	
	30		Returning from ARMENTIERES having completed course. bombs	
			Fine day. Exercise. bomb instruction	

Mod. Hudson A.
Capt
OC "A" Sqd. South Irish Horse

A. Sadra
L. i wa 2 sharr
vol: 4

121/7935

Army Form C. 2118.

WAR DIARY
or
INTELLIGENCE SUMMARY.
(*Erase heading not required.*)

Confidential

War Diary

of

"A" Sqn. South Irish Horse

from Dec 1. 1915 to Dec 31st 1915

Vol I

Army Form C. 2118.

WAR DIARY
INTELLIGENCE SUMMARY.
(Erase heading not required.)

of F Sqd SOUTH IRISH HORSE

Instructions regarding War Diaries and Intelligence Summaries are contained in F. S. Regs., Part II. and the Staff Manual respectively. Title pages will be prepared in manuscript.

Place	Date	Hour	Summary of Events and Information	Remarks and references to Appendices
STRAZEELE	1/12/15		Fine day. Exercises: 2nd Lieut. N. ANDERSON and 16 men go to ARMENTIERES to be attached to Cyclists to form a Catapult Battery.	21°/M
"	2/12/15		Fine day. Sqd Parade. Capt. J.M. WARDELL rejoined from Base after his illness	
	3/12/15		Wet day. Exercises. Bomb instruction	
	4/12/15		Wet day. Kit inspection. Camp routine	
	5/12/15		Church parade. Camp routine	
	6/12/15		Capt N. FURLONG & Capt. J.M. WARDELL go to ARMENTIERES to inspect Troop attached to R.P.M.	N.C.F.
	7/12/15		Sqd Parade. Fatigue men. Sqd exercise	
	8/12/15		Exercise. Camp routine. Bomb instruction	
	9/12/15		Very wet day. Exercise late on a/c of rain. Football in afternoon	
	10/12/15		Very wet Tuesday. Exercise. Lectures in dining room on bombs	
	11/12/15		Sqd parade. Football in afternoon	
	12/12/15		Church parade. Capt KIRK arrived	
	13/12/15		Fine day. Exercise bomb instruction. Horses for R.P.M. Troop arrived to draw four horses from Remount Scot rein from bad lot. Capt KIRK arrive.	
	14/12/15		Sqd parade. Camp routine. Capt KIRK declines to take them bomb instruction	
	15/12/15		D.A.D.R. & Major McDonnell A.D.V.S. 21 Divn. come to see Remount horses	

1577 Wt. W10791/1773 500,000 1/15 D. D. & L. A.D.S.S./Forms/C. 2118.

WAR DIARY
or
INTELLIGENCE SUMMARY

(Erase heading not required.)

Army Form C. 2118.

"A" Sqd South Irish Horse   21 OBW

Place	Date	Hour	Summary of Events and Information	Remarks and references to Appendices
STRAZEELE	16/2/15		In afternoon Capt. J.M. WADDELL & Lieut Fitzherbert take 16 men for his bomb throwing to Div. School at OUTERSTEENE exercise.	
	17/2/15		Exercise. Another 16 men (16 to OUTERSTEENE for bomb throwing Rain all day. Exercise Camp routine	
	18/2/15		Fine day. Sqd Parade. Football.	
	19/2/15		Church parade. Capt. C.P. Pratt to S.Amb. with bad Piles	M.P.S.
	20/2/15		Sqd parade. Lieut. J. VERNON goes to APPRENTICES to take Gas MASKS. Leaves. Lieut N.P. ANDERSON sick to Amb.	
	21/2/15		Rain all day. Exercise camp routine	
	22/2/15		Exercise. Bomb Instruction. Capt MPH Sheenet ANDERSON to Base Hospital. Leave allotment begins. 3 their weekly.	
	23/2/15		Sqd Parade. report to of the Cyclists that No.1068 P/S LARKIN F No.1073 P/S LE BAS L. No.1144 P/S SADLER P. W.A. No.1144 P/S SADLER P. W.A. was killed in action on night of 22/23" by direct hit of H.E. on the Catapult they were firing up to just Fine day. long exercise. Camp routine	N.C.A.
	24/2/15			
	25/2/15		Dinner day. Wet in morning: very good dinner for me	

Army Form C. 2118.

WAR DIARY
or
INTELLIGENCE SUMMARY
(Erase heading not required.)

"A" Sqdn South Irish Horse
21st Div

Place	Date	Hour	Summary of Events and Information	Remarks and references to Appendices
STRAZEELE	26/12/15		Fine day. Church parade. Exercise g/L.	
"	27/12/15		Fine day. Major McDonnell remonstrated with Mr MALLEN re Glanders. Reported to me by Lieut PEPPER that No. 477 Pte SHEPARD D.T. has been wounded on way to trenches. Send Kiss man to ARMENTIÈRES as reinforcements to Catapult battery. Horses unable to be moved on a/c of Mare testing.	A.A.I.
	28/12/15		Major McDonnell A.D.V.S. 21 Div. Came to see horses. No reactions all g/L. Well. I am dead to day. Light exercise	
	29/12/15		Fine day. Quite warm. Sqdn parade.	
	30/12/15		Fine day. Exercise. Bomb. instruction	
	31/12/15		Fine day. but windy. Sqdn parade. Sent Sergt Neill to Capt Vaugh to ARMENTIÈRES to receive instruction in use of Catapults in the trenches	

Noel Furlong.
Capt.
O/C "A" Sqdn South Irish Horse

21st Divisional Cavalry

"A" SQUADRON

SOUTH IRISH HORSE

JANUARY 1916

"A" Sp: S. Ind. Affrs
Vol: 5

21st

Army Form C. 2118.

WAR DIARY
or
INTELLIGENCE SUMMARY. "A" Sqn South IRISH Horse

(Erase heading not required.)

Instructions regarding War Diaries and Intelligence Summaries are contained in F. S. Regs., Part II. and the Staff Manual respectively. Title pages will be prepared in manuscript.

Place	Date	Hour	Summary of Events and Information	Remarks and references to Appendices
			Confidential

War Diary
of
"A" Sqn South Irish Horse

from Jan 1st 1916
to
Jan 31st 1916

Vol I | |

WAR DIARY
or
INTELLIGENCE SUMMARY.

(Erase heading not required.)

Army Form C. 2118.

Summary of Events and Information "A" Sqd. SOUTH IRISH HORSE

Place	Date	Hour	Summary of Events and Information	Remarks and references to Appendices
STRAZEELE	1/1/16		Fine day. Kit inspection. Foresees. Camp routine. Football in afternoon	
	2/1/16		Wet day. Camp routine. Church Parade	
	3/1/16		Fine. Foresees	
	4/1/16		Fine. Sqd. Parade	
	5/1/16		Fine. Foresees. Physical drill	
	6/1/16		Fine. do. Bomb instruction	
	7/1/16		Fine. Foresees. Map reading	
	8/1/16		Wet. Kit inspection. Foresees. Football	NCA
	9/1/16		Church Parade. Camp routine	
	10/1/16		Foresees. Bomb instruction	Issued point out that having
	11/1/16		Foresees. Camp routine. No 884 Pte SHANAHAN D. killed in action bff Catapult battery at ARMENTIERES. No 577 Pte WASSON A. wounded (Slight)	1 Off 16 men armr on Catapult battery leaves
	12/1/16		Full marching order Parade	
	13/1/16		do	18 horses saddles
	14/1/16		Sqd. Inspected by Lt. Col. JACOB. 21 "Div." Commander. He complimented Sqd. on Smart turn out & perfect condition of	its batty after trip. the horses

Army Form C. 2118.

WAR DIARY
or
INTELLIGENCE SUMMARY.

"A" Sqn South Irish Horse

(Erase heading not required.)

Place	Date	Hour	Summary of Events and Information	Remarks and references to Appendices
STRAZEELE	15/1/16		Camp Routine. Exercise.	Rest of Sqn and one troop away on potato duty. The men remaining have little else to do but stables
	16/1/16		Church Parade. Suit day.	
	17/1/16		Sqn Parade. bomb instruction	
	18/1/16		Rain all day. Exercise	
	19/1/16		Fine day. Exercise. map reading	
	20/1/16		Fine day. Exercise. Physical drill	
	21/1/16		Fine day. Sqn Parade	
	22/1/16		Fine day. Exercise. football	
	23/1/16		Church Parade. Very cold	
	24/1/16		Fine day. Saddle inspection. 2nd Lt D. HANRATTY	Exercise all Kit Part being taken out in the
	25/1/16		Joined Sqn from Base	A.O.L.
	26/1/16		Fine. Exercise. Camp Routine	
	27/1/16		Fine. Exercise. do	
	28/1/16		Fine. Exercise. Physical drill	
	29/1/16		Fine. Exercise. 2nd Lt. HAMILTON joined Rgt from Base	
	30/1/16		Fine. Tram. Exercise	
	31/1/16		Church Parade	Regt Tailor A Capt A Sqn S.I. Horse
	31/1/16		Fine. Exercise	O/c A Sqn S.I. Horse

21st Divisional Cavalry

"A" SQUADRON

SOUTH IRISH HORSE

FEBRUARY 1916

A. Seward
S. I. House
21st Dec.
Vol. 6.

Army Form C. 2118.

WAR DIARY
or
INTELLIGENCE SUMMARY.

(Erase heading not required.)

Confidential

War Diary
of
"A" Sqn. South Irish Horse

From Feb 1st 1916
Feb 29th 1916

Army Form C. 2118.

WAR DIARY
or
INTELLIGENCE SUMMARY.

(Erase heading not required.)

Instructions regarding War Diaries and Intelligence Summaries are contained in F. S. Regs., Part II. and the Staff Manual respectively. Title pages will be prepared in manuscript.

Place	Date	Hour	Summary of Events and Information	Remarks and references to Appendices
STAZEELE	1/2/16		Fine. Cold. Camp Routine. exercise "A" Coy South Irish Horse	
	2/2/16		Frost very cold. Capt. T.M. WARDELL sent to APPRENTIEPES to take over Catapult battery from Lieut Fitzherbert. Exercise	
	3/2/16		Fine. Cold. Kit inspection. exercise	
	4/2/16		Very cold. Camp Routine. exercise	
	5/2/16		Fine. Exercise. Instruction in bomb throwing for recruits	
	6/2/16		Fine. Church Parade. Camp routine	
	7/2/16		Rain. Exercise. Pay day.	
	8/2/16		Fine. Exercise. Physical drill	
	9/2/16		Fine. Exercise. Rifle practice on miniature range	
	10/2/16		do do	
	11/2/16		Rain rain. Exercise. kit inspection.	
	12/2/16		Fine. Exercise. Catapult battery under Capt T.M. WARDELL threw bombs in PONT BALLOT Salient	
	13/2/16		Fine. Church Parade	

Army Form C. 2118.

WAR DIARY
or
INTELLIGENCE SUMMARY.
(Erase heading not required.)

Instructions regarding War Diaries and Intelligence Summaries are contained in F. S. Regs., Part II. and the Staff Manual respectively. Title pages will be prepared in manuscript.

Place	Date	Hour	Summary of Events and Information "A" Sqn South Irish Horse	Remarks and references to Appendices
STAZEELE	14/2/16		Very wet day. exercise in afternoon. Camp routine	
	15/2/16		Snow. too bad for exercise. Pickets on outposts	
	16/2/16		Snow. made ring in yard for exercise	
	17/2/16		Snow. exercise in field. Camp routine	
	18/2/16		Snow. do	
	19/2/16		Snow. Catapult battery threw Newton bombs in trench 80	
	20/2/16		Snow. Church parade. Camp routine	
	21/2/16		Fair. exercise in field. Pay day	
	22/2/16		Snow again. do	
	23/2/16		do do	
	24/2/16		Catapult battery threw Newton bombs in trench 73, during bombardment. Camp routine	
	25/2/16		Snow - Camp Routine & exercise	
	26/2/16		do do	
	27/2/16		do Church Parade. Camp routine	

Place	Date	Hour	Summary of Events and Information	Remarks and references to Appendices
MAREUIL	28/2/16		Quiet. Proceeded in field kit inspection.	A Sqn South Irish Horse
	29/2/16		Quiet. Exercise. Camp Routine. During this month I had - 30 men & 1 off attached to RHQ for duties took, and 16 men & 1 off. forming a Catapult battery. This left me with Horses & Home times four horses per man. and I could do nothing but stakes to keep them in exercise.	

H.S.E. Fairtlough
Capt.
O/C A Sqn South Irish Horse

21st Divisional Cavalry

"A" SQUADRON

SOUTH IRISH HORSE

MARCH 1916

21ˢᵗ Nov

"A" S.I. Hope

Vol 7

Army Form C. 2118.

WAR DIARY
or
INTELLIGENCE SUMMARY.

(Erase heading not required.)

Confidential

WAR DIARY

"A" Sqn South Irish Horse

from March 1st 1916 to March 31st 1916

Army Form C. 2118.

WAR DIARY
or
INTELLIGENCE SUMMARY.
(Erase heading not required.)

A Sqd South Irish Horse

Instructions regarding War Diaries and Intelligence Summaries are contained in F. S. Regs., Part II. and the Staff Manual respectively. Title pages will be prepared in manuscript.

Place	Date	Hour	Summary of Events and Information	Remarks and references to Appendices
STAZEELE	1/3/16		Suis. Sqdrs football in afternoon	
"	2/3/16		— Sqds Parade. Kit inspection in afternoon	
"	3/3/16		— Exercise. Catapult Battery at APREMPIERES	
"	4/3/16		— up for combined attack at trench 50.	
"	5/3/16		Snow all day. Sqdr routine	
"	6/3/16		— Church Parade	
"	7/3/16		Snow & frost. Kit inspection. Lectures on Care of Horses	
"	8/3/16		Very cold. Sqdrs routine	
"	9/3/16		Suis. Sqds parade. Sqdr routine	
"	10/3/16		Suis. Exercise. Sqdr routine	
"	11/3/16		Suis. Rifles inspection exercise	
"	12/3/16		Very cold. Wind & rain. Lectures on outposts	
"	13/3/16		Church Parade. Football in afternoon	
"			Very fine & warm. 2 Lieuts HAMILTON & HAM RATTY	

WAR DIARY or INTELLIGENCE SUMMARY

Army Form C. 2118.

(Erase heading not required.)

4th Sqdn South Irish Horse

Place	Date	Hour	Summary of Events and Information	Remarks and references to Appendices
STAZEELE	14/3/16		Very windy day. 2nd Lieut Hanratty rejoined Sqdn after course of instruction with 2 Can Div. Capt Fowling flies. Sqdn parade.	
	15/3/16		Sqdn Exercise. football in afternoon	
	16/3/16		Sqdn Exercise. Kit inspection	
	17/3/16		St Patrick's day. holiday to men. 30 men attached to H.Q.N. & 16 men of B. Catapult battery. re-joined H.E. Sqdn	
	18/3/16		Windy. Troop drill. Capt Fowling's exercise. Landed on beaten vehicles	
	19/3/16		Fine. Church Parade	
	20/3/16		Fine. Exercise horses. re arranging Sqd working out troops etc. with an order to B for Course of instruction to 2 Can Div. for 14 days	
	21/3/16		Fine. Sqd parade. Rural outpost scheme	
	22/3/16		Rain. Landing in entire Rd. Capt Fowling	

Army Form C. 2118.

WAR DIARY
or
INTELLIGENCE SUMMARY.
(Erase heading not required.)

1/1 South Irish Horse

Instructions regarding War Diaries and Intelligence Summaries are contained in F. S. Regs., Part II. and the Staff Manual respectively. Title pages will be prepared in manuscript.

Place	Date	Hour	Summary of Events and Information	Remarks and references to Appendices
STAZEELE	23/3/16		Cold rain. Camp routine. Horse to be tob for the Cavalry.	
	24/3/16		Quiet. Exercise. Wet inspection.	
	25/3/16		Saw . small refining.	
	26/3/16		Church Parade.	
	27/3/16		Sur. Sgts Parade.	
	28/3/16		Sur. Sgts inspected by Gen. Plumer. Command up.	
			2nd Army.	
	29/3/16		Exercise. Camp routine.	
	30/3/16		Recive orders to move on 4/4/16 to XIII Corps	
			Exercise.	
	31/3/16		Arranging for move.	

Noel Lusborne
Capt.
O/c "A" Sqn. South Irish Horse

21st Divisional Cavalry

Became part of XV Corps Cavalry in MAY 1916

"A" SQUADRON

SOUTH IRISH HORSE

APRIL 1916

Army Form C. 2118.

WAR DIARY
or
INTELLIGENCE SUMMARY.
(Erase heading not required.)

A Sqd South Irish Horse Vol 8

Place	Date	Hour	Summary of Events and Information	Remarks and references to Appendices
STAAZEELE	1/4/16		Entrained HQ Sqd at GODEWAERSVELDE Station at 5. P.M.	
	2/4/16		Detrained HQ Sqd at LONGUEAU Station at 7.30 A.M. after breakfast baters [?] marched to PIBEMONT ? with HQ Sqn joined XIII Corps. Went into billets	
PIBEMONT	3/4/16		Very hot day. Camp routines. rested Sqds after journey	
	4/4/16		Cold. Camp Routines. Lieut Fitzherbert training 12 men	
	5/4/16		to the Div. Outposts Lt. VERNON acts as Camp Commandant	
	6/4/16		Cold. Training Outposts	do
	7/4/16		do	do
	8/4/16		do	
	9/4/16		Sing Sam Kit inspection. Foremans football in P.M.	
	9/4/16		Church Parade. Camp routines	
	10/4/16		Duts. Foremans Training Outposts	

Army Form C. 2118.

WAR DIARY
or
INTELLIGENCE SUMMARY. "A" (D) Scott Irish Horse

(Erase heading not required.)

Instructions regarding War Diaries and Intelligence Summaries are contained in F. S. Regs., Part II. and the Staff Manual respectively. Title pages will be prepared in manuscript.

Place	Date	Hour	Summary of Events and Information	Remarks and references to Appendices
PIEDMONT	11/4/16		Cold rain. Exercise. Camp routine	
	12/4/16		Rain all day. All men & Officers recalled off leave	
	13/4/16		Exercise in morning. Exercise musketry on range in P.M.	
	14/4/16		Rain. Sqd parade in morn & musketry in P.M.	
	15/4/16		Rain. Exercise. Football in afternoon	
	16/4/16		Rain. Church Parade. Camp routine	
	17/4/16		Warm. Exercises. Sent 3 horses & 2 men to be attached to No. 9 R.L.O. Sqd.	
	18/4/16		Rain all day. Kit inspection in billets	
	19/4/16		Rain all day. Exercises.	
	20/4/16		Rough rain. Sqd Parade	
	21/4/16		Fine morning. Exercises. Recce. Col Duvall Returned. Musketry in P.M.	
	22/4/16		Fine morning. Success musketry. Recce. het P.M.	
	23/4/16		Easter Sund. Very fine. Church Parade.	

WAR DIARY or INTELLIGENCE SUMMARY

Army Form C. 2118.

Place	Date	Hour	Summary of Events and Information	Remarks and references to Appendices
Fitz Herbert	24/4/16		This day 2nd Lieut HERBERT & Lieut VIPROW promoted Capt. from March 1st. A Sqd South Irish Horse	
	25/4/16		Capt from March 1st. Capt FITZHERBERT & 12 men to Tievelos as Suresomed Serjeant. First day Lieut HAM PATTY & 30 men attached to A.P.M for instruction in road control; 60 men for special fatigue 5.P.M to 11.30 P.M unloading R.E. stores.	
	26/4/16		do	
	27/4/16		do	
	28/4/16		Exercise. Coup routine. police & serjeants	
	29/4/16		do	
	30/4/16		Church Parade	

Noel Sutton
Capt.
Commanding

21st Divisional Cavalry

XV Corps Cavalry

Left 21st Division & joined XV Corps 14.5.16

"A" SQUADRON

SOUTH IRISH HORSE

MAY 1916

Army Form C. 2118.

"A" S.I. HQrs Vol 9

WAR DIARY
or
INTELLIGENCE SUMMARY.
(Erase heading not required.)

Confidential

War Diary

"A" Sqn South Irish Horse

May 1st 1916 to May 31st 1916

Army Form C. 2118.

WAR DIARY
or
INTELLIGENCE SUMMARY.
(Erase heading not required.)

"A" Sqd South Irish Horse

Instructions regarding War Diaries and Intelligence Summaries are contained in F.S. Regs., Part II. and the Staff Manual respectively. Title pages will be prepared in manuscript.

Place	Date	Hour	Summary of Events and Information	Remarks and references to Appendices
Ribemont	1/5/16		30 men attached A.P.M. bill office, for police work. Mrs H Capt A.V. F.B. Asphet & 12 men in trenches as 21" Divisional Suitzers Peronne ale Caut Poelcus	
	2/5/16		do	
	3/5/16		—	
	4/5/16		—	
	5/5/16		Move out of billets to lines in wood	
	6/5/16		—	
	7/5/16		Church Parade	
	8/5/16		as on 1st instant	
	9/5/16		orders received that Div. Cav. is to cross & that Hr Sqd XV Corps & storm trail is to move to XV Corps & Polies & Suppers with dress — good hay way Moved into lines & tents — wet night between Ribemont & Heilly. Caut Poeting setting officers down C Sqd Suffey & Yeomanry arrive to form had of Reg	
	10/5/16			
	11/5/16			

Army Form C. 2118.

WAR DIARY
or
INTELLIGENCE SUMMARY.

(Erase heading not required.)

"A" Sqn South Irish Horse

Instructions regarding War Diaries and Intelligence Summaries are contained in F. S. Regs., Part II. and the Staff Manual respectively. Title pages will be prepared in manuscript.

Place	Date	Hour	Summary of Events and Information	Remarks and references to Appendices
La Tues	12/5/16		1 Regt. 12 men to G.S. Escort IV Corps Commander.	
Lof Wad			1 Regt. 11 men to be attached IV Corps H.Q.	
Wazee				
Pissitart	13/5/16		Regt. wet Camp Pouting	
Herrely	14/5/16		Church parade. "B" Sqn South Irish Horse under Command Major Stepn arrives + inspects the IV Corps Cav. Regt.	
	15/5/16		Major Stepn takes temp Command). Capt. F.H. Wadden acting adj. Camp Pouting	
	16/5/16		do. Parades under Major Stepn scheme.	
	17/5/16		Regtl.	
	18/5/16		Camp Pouting	
	19/5/16		do. Capt. Furlow & Jas Amiens to see a play t/a.P.M. 21 pr.	
	20/5/16		Horse. Church parade. Orders received that "C" Sqn Reverly Geo attd. to peace IV Corps Cav Regt. to be replaced by "D" Sqn Wilts Yeo with Headqrs Compts under Lt. Col. Ulric Thynne.	

Army Form C. 2118.

WAR DIARY
or
INTELLIGENCE SUMMARY
(Erase heading not required.)

A Sqn South Irish Horse

Place	Date	Hour	Summary of Events and Information	Remarks and references to Appendices
In Lines lay back between PLOEGSTEERT & HEILLY	22/5/16		Lt Col Wm T.C. THYNNE takes over Command of the Regt. left his Wilts Yeo H.Q.S. Regt. now consists of Sqn: "A" Sqn South Irish Horse. "B" Sqn do. "D" Sqn Wilts Yeo. Working party of 30 men at BRAY digging.	
	23/5/16		Regtl Parade for last by O.C's Command.	
	24/5/16		Rest at S.H. owing to return it's Horsemans.	
	25/5/16		Regtl Parade + Inspection by O.C's Command.	
	26/5/16		1 N.C.O. + 12 men O.C's Command Escort " " " A.P.M. IV Corps	
	27 "		30 men working party do BRAY	
	28 "		do Church Parade	
	29 "		Working party do Noel Newton a	
	30 "		do do	Cpl "A" Sqn
	31 "		do do	Corp. "B" Sqn South Irish Horse

www.ingramcontent.com/pod-product-compliance
Lightning Source LLC
Chambersburg PA
CBHW081245170426
43191CB00037B/2050